Male Pattern

poems by

Gus Peterson

Finishing Line Press
Georgetown, Kentucky

Male Pattern

Copyright © 2025 by Gus Peterson
ISBN 979-8-89990-002-0 First Edition
All rights reserved under International and Pan-American Copyright Conventions. No part of this book may be reproduced in any manner whatsoever without written permission from the publisher, except in the case of brief quotations embodied in critical articles and reviews.

ACKNOWLEDGMENTS

First, to the luxury of having too many voices to thank. You are the best most untragic chorus of direct and slant. Without you this wouldn't be. Any creation is the end result of a collective effort. Thank you, you who—if I've gone about this right—know who you are.

Second, everlasting gratitude to whomever familiarized me with the phrase n-of-1, which has and continues to be more useful than you'll ever know. It is the essence of what follows, which is a singular experience among billions and should never be taken as a prescription for one's own n-of-1 being. You do you. And may the world be better —and love you—for it.

Publisher: Leah Huete de Maines
Editor: Christen Kincaid
Cover Art: Carol K. Peterson
Author Photo: Carol K. Peterson
Cover Design: Elizabeth Maines McCleavy

Order online: www.finishinglinepress.com
also available on amazon.com

Author inquiries and mail orders:
Finishing Line Press
PO Box 1626
Georgetown, Kentucky 40324
USA

Contents

I
- The Way 1
- After the Rain 2
- Putting it Off 3
- Old Piano 4
- The Stars 5
- Crane Fly 6
- The Weeding 8

II
- Nest 11
- Robin 12
- Maple Season 13
- In the Photo 14
- A Long Dead Spider 16
- Lobster Boat 17
- Lines Composed in a Former Church 18
- Spring Noir 19

III
- Fringe 23
- Meditations on an Overturned 18-Wheeler 24
- Hand Axe 26
- This Unsettled Pattern 27
- Dermatology 28
- Dave 29
- Grackle 30
- The Plans 31

IV
- Heart Monitor 35
- Red or White 36
- "Mathura Man Sets Record by Staring at Sun for Over an Hour" ... 37
- Fine Print 38
- Schrödinger's Office 39
- Before Deciding 40
- Humidity 41
- Power Outage: Office 42

Like the Stem of a Thought Bubble 43
Impressionism... 44
Jazz.. 45

V
Fog... 49
Diagnosis: Eye Strain 50
MRI 51
Trouble Letting Go 52
Going Back on the Pills 53
Strange Look 54
October 55
Male Pattern Baldness.. 56

VI
it is what it is.. 59
On Halloween 60
Remodeling 61
Stone Age 62
Having it Out with Winter 63
December Moon... 65
Mother is a Verb, too.. 66

VII
Relax... 69
Braiding the Challah 70
February... 71
Rerouted 72
The Handshake 74
I, too, Love Lucy 75
Henge 77
Bodybuilder... 78
Another Dollar Store... 79

for Carol, who makes possible the impossible

I

The Way

The Way

The way,
if you've bitten
your lip, your tongue,
you keep biting it.
The way the scarlet
of every scab winks,
voluptuous red button.
The way the world
mines enough salt,
squeezes just enough
juice from a lemon
for the small cuts.
The way paper
holds this poem,
is sometimes
the knife.

After the Rain

I want to tell how the sun came out,
how the pelt of new grass
steamed like an exhaustion of fur
as birds sang, peopled telephone wires.
Not how it kept topping itself off the way
you fill glass after glass with cola,
that delicate negotiation of lather
and peace. Then the meniscus of a river
couldn't contain its enthusiasm,
and the grocery store became perishable,
a beach resort, water lapping at trolleys,
the loading dock a pier, its shelving
an ebbing tide. And I wish the news van,
its giant ear turned to the sky's low
angry bristle, showed up for the progress
we've made, reinventing the main
street of this forgotten municipality,
that the parking lot they filmed
held more than the dark tracer fire
of fish across its mosaic of lines.
How, on the way out of town,
two women were sitting on a blanket
beside the torrent. How they passed
a thermos back and forth, just watched
that rage so ready to sweep them
off their feet, already kissing faces
with such cold tenderness.

Putting it Off

All week the industriousness of others pawed
your window, pets let in and out, out and in.

Some days it is all you can do, reducing mountains
of laundry to rubble. Years ago, backpacking a spine

of peaks strung like clothesline across this state,
you learned how to move for days looking down.

Learned the lie of ascent, its mirage of summits.
The way an empty riverbed mulches underfoot.

Kneeling beside the puddle, a definition of thirst.
How the body overrides, wants what it wants.

This plodding you're doing now, out to the shed,
the mower gasping a disappointed resuscitation.

Old Piano

We move it like tugboats
through the kitchen
and outside onto the deck.
Between efforts one of us
bends over and sways,
the rest leaning like dames,
elbows against lacquered wood,
beers in hand, melancholy notes
flung out over the dusky yard
like feed for the chickens.
It's last call and soon
we'll fill its box with earth
and it will tilt like a headstone
against the fence, but the children
still practice, quietly between chores,
a riot of fingers on soundless keys
though a new Steinway grins
in the den, and long after the peepers
have sung out their loneliness,
when new flowers cascade
their own sheet music down,
they'll brush the blooms
aside and play.

The Stars

We say to them: wish upon one
knowing it is dust and echoes.
We press small muzzle flashes
of yellow and gold onto quizzes
and report cards for what we call
good behavior, say when a piece
of the sky falls it is shooting,
shoot the sky when overcome
with the killable joy that is
our brass jacketed truth riddling
flesh and bone, a failed test.
Look up. They're still there,
waiting, row upon row of them,
in a desk drawer of the teacher.
How, how do constellations come
from this cemetery of light,
the shot through night?

Crane Fly

> *"People call them giant mosquitoes, but these gentle giants are not mosquitoes at all."*
> —University of Arizona Cooperative Extension, March 6, 2020

When it first landed, I was not conflicted.
What amber could contain such monstrosity?

Yet it was not seeking blood. Only rest.
Perhaps it was the book I had just finished

where a rip in the fabric of spacetime
allows a hungry insect to drink a brain

the way we once emptied skull after skull
of coconut on vacation, eyes closed,

plastic proboscises sating salt crusted lips.
It could have been, or maybe it was

the malaria of loss, possibility buzzing
its insistent cloud as you sat in bed solving

puzzle after puzzle, both of us waiting,
the IV's long water slide comically red.

The way *transfusion* and *hemoglobin* rolled
like hardened candy around our mouths.

Tell me, was it me painting the catalog
model's pristine face with its sheer wing,

me who left one leg fine as your hair
plastered to the wall's white wash?

My heart quickened when an hour later
it dragged its wreckage onto my desk?

As it paused, twitching, I couldn't help it:
I'm sorry. I'm sorry. As if it could forgive.

What else to say? Isn't any mercy also salve
for one who fabricates the need for it?

The Weeding

I could tell you something, reader,
something about coaxing seedlings
out of the world's rough furrow,
but she knows her garden,
too close now to the embrace
of dirt to break her back for it.
She struts up and down each rank,
each file of vegetable and herb
like a glorious general, correcting,
nodding approvals as the boys lean over
and grab, young muscles straining,
hungry for the snap, a head separating
from the stem of its neck or,
if done the way she showed them,
the whole body surrendered,
roots and all.

II

Nest

Nest

Because it's spring it warms enough
to be outside. And because it is outside
you need to hack some sort of order from
its wilderness, and so you unlock the
barn doors to the shed and it disgorges
all the apparatus you need to accomplish
this manifest destiny—a weed whacker,
the chortling mower, loppers and shears.
And because you are suddenly so pastoral
you are on the porch, a porch you built
off the side of the shed thinking you would
accomplish the writing of more poems,
and because you thought you would spend
time here you put in a pool and two rocking
chairs to sit on in case you have company.
And because of all this you are sweeping
the grit of winter away from the floor
and positioning the chairs like you've seen
in home makeover shows, quaintly rustic.
And now you've forgotten to prune the lilac
again, so it has become wild, almost feral,
a neglect so large it begins to list and tear
itself apart. And the birds who have cloistered
in its arms for generations move elsewhere,
all of them except one family who have woven
a home of its bloom and branch into an eave
you sit under, rocking because you're older
now and understand why people in the country
have porches and lullabying chairs to settle into,
when all the chores are done and the end
of a day comes sooner than expected.

Robin

Perhaps the website's description
of the plumage—
rust—is most accurate,
the male's brighter, more corrosive.
Only the male, it continues,
sings *cheerily, cheer up* he says
to the morning, to the dusk,
when it's about to rain.
Cheer up.

Maple Season

Early spring,
snow's wet laundry
in the fields,
waiting to be hung.
In old woods
the tinny blink
of kicked buckets
bloodletting.
For years the one
out front how
grandmothers knew
the bushy brow
of a storm was coming—
its toothy turned faces,
open slap of wind.
It saps so much,
distilling any loss
to a sweetness.
Last year the last
shook its fallen hands
into shaking piles.
How red they were.
As if burned by a sun.
As if never having
known shade.

In the Photo

My father's father is preaching,
one palm raised, the book he believed
was the language of creation
held reverently in his hand the way
one cradles a dying thing close,
those long fingers that could sunder
the small, hardened brain of a walnut
to soft meat caressing its leather.
Did he hold my wailing head
this fervently, my supple skull
crammed with its nascent folding
of blank pages? Every time I feel
an urge to pray I remember touching
his icy, powdered face. My sister
ensconced in that highchair of arms.
Her kindergartener's grief. For weeks
I bunked in the bubble gum pink cathedral
of her room, mine so foggy with death
a mural of sailboats across one wall bobbed
atop its water. There on a tide of sheets
my father's father slipped out to sea,
eating the bread of himself until
only a heart shadowed the memory
of body. I didn't understand his desire
to not taste then, why every morning
my mother placed each fresh temptation
of apple atop that book like an offering
to the bed. The vigils the living keep.
I kissed the crackling parchment of his hand
before school, snuck the gift pressed
to my palm like forbidden knowledge
onto a teacher's desk. What isn't written
about any genesis is how quiet it is
after a flood. The way the skies clear.
Just a few days ago that sodden cradle
in the street had rocked its newborn,
the rain falling and falling outside.
I want to say to him: do not preach
to me of doves. I want to know why

they drowned, lullabies in their mouths.
Why any faithful disciple still follows
the light of their only sun, even after
it absconds from heaven.

A Long Dead Spider

Little arachnoid planet
I find you at the end of your thread
hung like a birdcage
in the bathroom after a shower.
Little mountaineer, little climber,
there is already so much death.
Why belay ourselves?
The way back is granite hard.
I hoist you like a fish
to pale yellow vanity light.
Little jumper, did you leap
with good intention?
Always a ball of string
in your belly to slow the fall.
Did you starve half full?
If, at the end, I hugged
myself eight times,
I might too.

Lobster Boat

Miles from the coast
and I see you,
nameless shipwreck,
about fifty feet in
from this road where traps
moonlight as décor.
A perfect storm,
the way we clammed up,
became moored,
forgot the taste of salt,
the tuning of your heart.
How cages are hauled up
one at a time.

Lines Composed in a Former Church

Isn't this a kind of prayer,
how we congregate in a waiting area,
heads bowed, the good word drilled
all around? Stained glass gone, the saints
still comfort us, coveralled and bent.
How easily apertures to sanctity converted
to another bay door, a whale's impossible mouth
swallowing each Jonah bumper to bumper.
Tell me, does salvation still ask regular maintenance?
Is hourly labor rate a tithe? Because it remains
miraculous, our broken and sick made well.
Still faith, whatever is left to blackened hands,
the way we pass the keys over, are called
to worship whenever there's a knock
under the hood.

Spring Noir

Startled into grey dawn,
for a moment you lie nameless,
John Doe toes sticking up
from a tangle of white sheet.
Then, like the rain
falling softly from the eaves,
life drips back into
the opened vein of your mind—
how it was that dolls and jazz
slipping its boozy arm
around your heart at night
became a shadow wreathed
in the breath of street vents,
the voice uttered from mouths
of dark alley, a river of fedora
coursing soaked streets,
pulled low so no one ever
solves the case.

III

Fringe

Fringe

Flesh to this hardened artery of concrete,
its green plaques of ingress and egress,
the vena cava of villages and towns
around what we term a city in this state.
Where the woods fray like a first rank
of an assaulting force tumbled ashore,
sturdy leg trunks felled like trees,
every projectile a widow maker,
a stopped heart, outermost feather
of a breaker frothing up sand.
Here long grass and sumac stipple
and animals arrive, like beachgoers—
throngs of whitetail, troupes of turkeys,
the Tom lifeguarding, his courtesan fan
a whistle of asphalt preventing colors.
They thread out as from a rug, eating.
Today driving in I glimpse a loping fox,
think of that tail sweeping some man's neck
in centuries gone, inverted yield signs
of ear perched atop the post of his head,
listening. How the deer sheltered his
chest and arms, seams of their chest
strung like prayer flags from wrist
to shoulder, the outside of a leg.
That herd of hyphens, subtractions
and passing lanes moving as he moved,
a windblown forest slipped through
its forest, hunting itself.

Meditations on an Overturned 18-Wheeler

I.

When they met, she could not tell him
how she hauled those long nights.

II.

From dark a coyote confesses himself.
The headlight of the old man glares down.
Forgive me, father.

III.

This Venn diagram of illuminating.
See the endless perforations passing,
sawing its periphery?

IV.

True loneliness
  requires
a series
  of small shifts
to accelerate
  back
into the flow
  of traffic.

V.

Anything proffered to the wind flies
given enough momentum.

VI.

Rorschach test in red:
Bandit tale. Quilt of quills.
Ninth life. Man's best friend.

VII.

In time this air you trust
leaves you jackknifed,
rivers of dark fruit spilling
onto the pavement.

VIII.

Shotgun under the seat.
Shotgun an emptiness riding
passenger across leaden days.

IX.

Twitch, Wombat, Large Marge.
Toe Jam, Fat Cat, Rusty Nail.
Scrap King, Hard to Carry.

X.

We pulled imaginary strings.
And like a southward flock
of geese the world honks
before passing us by.

Hand Axe

An old farmer walks
into the archaeology lab
with it tucked under his arm
as if the gray stone were
another roll of chicken wire,
and I envy that gruff way
of absorbing astonishments,
want to be more annoyed like him
at having to mend the fence again,
to shed parts of myself the way
grazing land sloughs into a creek
after a week of nonstop rain.
And if I am to linger, let me remain
sharp as knapped ice age blades,
or at least undisturbed as a Holstein
slaking its thirst while something
misplaced for two or three millennia
is pulled with a grunt
like a weed from the ground.

This Unsettled Pattern

Will continue for the foreseeable
future, the weatherman says,
waving his hand wearily
at the blank wall behind him,
the doppler on our screens
a churn, an uneasy stomach.
At first it was funny as you recovered
from surgery, to know no one
was swimming or splashing,
how the public pool sat placid
or riddled with a tommy gun of drops,
all the grills and furniture covered,
estates made ready for auction.
How, at times, a warning rumble
would issue from its scuffed gray throat
though there was no one to threaten.
Then your geraniums that survived frost
were frosted black with fungus,
ice kept rattling up the throat
of its dying refrigeration.
If spring was baking, summer
is a convection of citrus and acid,
its yard a too wet sponge, loaf
after loaf of green, envious bread.
Isn't that how any world ends,
part thirst, part underwater,
snared in ligatures of smoke?
How to tell if this haze is after life
or afterlife? I can't help it,
the fireworks last night
were so vibrant, as if piped
by some chef's giant, steady hand
before the weeping sky consumed them
and sweetness melted like sugar
back into the opened mouths
of upturned eyes.

Dermatology

Your nurse, Shelly, is new here,
as Briana was six months before.
Faces turning over like skin cells,
like a shark's Rolodex of teeth.
Maybe it's these four ashen walls,
each with its own cancer poster.
Maybe someone can only gaze
at the sad lumpy pillow of a body,
unsheathed from its case of cotton
and polyester, for so long. No doubt
she already sees the way the afghan
of your largest organ will stretch
and fray with time, its rents and runs.
But she is kind, humming a wordless
tune to you as the doctor inserts a needle
into the darkening period on your neck.
He shaves the mole and even though
you're supposed to feel nothing you think
of the Mars rover, millions of miles distant,
scraping bits of a planet into similar tubes
for analysis. How it didn't have a Shelly,
sang happy birthday to itself as it worked.
That was years ago, when freckles reminded
you of constellations. When you looked up
and imagined what looking back was.

Dave

We used to wonder
about him, sitting out
on the sunny steps eating
sardines on cracker,
watching the birds,
strolling up the road
for a coffee even though
the pot burbled all day
upstairs, trimming his Bonsai
between sales calls,
popping the weathered text
of his features into offices
instead of email.
We learned to seal off
any openings, to pick up
the phone whenever
his boots approached.
Seven years gone
and here we are,
still talking behind
closed doors.

Grackle

Something has gone missing.
They line up in formation
and grid the freshly mown grass,
iridescent and polished as sheriffs
preening for hungry cameras.
And I can't help but watch
this search like these stricken mothers,
heart spiking every time one
bends over, pecks at the ground.
It is late July and drought
renders everything a boneyard.
On our TV a tired woman presses
her face into the opened book
of her hands. *I've run out
of tears,* she says.

The Plans

1. Spoiler

Even the best laid are subject to change.

2. Etymology

To/Some/Week/One/Sun/day.
God-willing/Weather-permitting.
Let's/Make/Circle/Date/Calendar.
If/When/Things/Go/Right.

3. Empire

Ask the Greek. Ask the Roman.
Over there—see, in the museum?
The marble one still poised
as if lightning were in
his hand.

4. New iPhone

Scroll to the end and check agree.
These are your terms and conditions.

5. Reno

Caesarstone. Hardwood.
Lazy Susan. A soft touch close.
The architect draws a blueprint.
The body issues its permit.

6. Second Spoiler

Where there was a mass, nothing.
Where there is nothing, a pantry.
You may use it more, or less.
It will shine and sparkle.
It is still a kitchen.

IV

Heart Monitor

Heart Monitor

It's my first stint with cardiology
but she's seen me before.
Seventy-two hours, she says,
voice unrolling like a bolt
of low notes. *Don't get it wet—
no showers, no swimming,
don't exercise too hard—
but we want you to go about
your life as normally as possible,*
she adds, shaving a few hairs
from my chest, taping electrodes
over my cubicle of ribs. A device
is hung from my neck like a medal
and I notice though her name
starts with a T she initials her
paperwork with the symbol
for Pi. *I love numbers,* she says,
plugging in the wires,
and recites only the first
dozen numerals after 3.14,
because there's another patient
behind me and the odds—
I'm not a doctor, mind you—
of something broken at my age
are less than what I'd like
them to be.

Red or White

Despite your best efforts
they will come, the thoughts,
despite bottle after bottle
poured down the gullet
as companion to cuisine,
to medication, as the three
course feast of itself.
Despite all that they arrive
like a dinner guest with bread
and an opinion about what
pairs best with this,
with that concerned look
that says *I'm not here for
your attempt at Coq Au Vin,*
despite it they will sit,
and chew, will send small
petty gossip like bats across
the twilight of candles,
will always seem on
the cusp of uncorking,
will raise a glass, will sip,
and sip, and sip, *salud*
and *bon appetit* dripped
from mouths like fat
off the bone.

"Mathura Man Sets Record by Staring at Sun for Over an Hour"

Seventy and retired
it comes to this—
apertures white as snow,
the comforting dark.
Out of sight, out of mind.
The tired engine's bark
and burp of black
fireworks he saw explode
once like a profusion
of lotus across night.
And this summer's
sun softened streets?
Cool river mud
between boyhood toes.
He does this unblinking.
Because it hurts,
the light that bounces
off this world.
We squint and squint,
trying to adjust,
not so much to shut out
as look past it.

Fine Print

> *"Immortal age beside immortal youth*
> *And all I was, in ashes."*
> —Alfred Lord Tennyson, "Tithonus"

As in no, you may not
wish for more wishes.

As in asked to live forever.
As in not forever young.

As in metamorphose
to three legs, then six.

As in Monkey's Paw
wintered to a fist.

As in it never dies,
her sleepless summer

dark. Its hot breath.
And that cicada shriek

for release, perhaps love,
that too will linger on

like a moonlit shadow
over the sound of crickets.

As in disquieting silence
or the male, seeking.

Schrödinger's Office

I'm thinking of time, or the way
you said a *quarter century*.
How it sagged against one
of four walls, sunk like a rock
to the bottom of the break room.
We were speaking of this place,
its right angles and ghostly fluorescence.
If only we too could regenerate
with a fresh coat of paint or a new
row of windows winking in sunlight,
things would be different.
If only those stairs were less steep.
For half a half century we've clattered
inside this box like the shaken
contents of a yet unwrapped present,
living the gift of half-lives.
As if we were ever all there
to begin with.

Before Deciding

Get up and wonder if showering once a week counts
as successful behavior activation. Don't shower.
Drive to the job your therapist says is killing you.
Yes, you are lonely enough to open that email
from the LinkedIn recruiter, to check profiles
of every duck lipped bot who friend requests.
Google exploding head syndrome, hypnagogic jerks,
all the nocturnal ways your tired body emulates
that first day of your first summer job in high school
when, sweeping up the jobsite, you brushed a live wire.
When your wife calls, ask what she wants for dinner.
If she pings the question back in that *are you okay* sonar,
featureless and cold as an empty plate, suggest leftovers.
Pouring coffee remember to pick up her prescription.
Tattoo its reminder on your hand in the same red ink
your boss uses to remind you. Google forgetfulness
again. Recall googling is not a positive coping skill.
Try to focus with progressive muscle relaxation.
As you clench and release, watch the sun drop
into another boiling evening like an egg.
How the tines of a tree spill its yolk
just before darkness.

Humidity

A still life day, but nothing paints.
Perspiration in your shirt,
in the trees, slung over a lake.
As quick as it clears it
reforms, spray of bullets
between the wiper's metronome.
Like your spring ambitions
in a flowerbed, dry and lifeless.
They lean, gaunt and brown,
everything sponged from them
into the air, who can't decide
where to lay all its grief.

Power Outage: Office

None of us knows how
to make small talk.

So we watch the rain loosen
its tie, begin a slow sashay.

All week grey hung
like a low angry fruit.

Now every window weeps,
is a taped off crime scene.

Horns in the distance—
traffic lights are down.

One by one we drain
our link to the collective.

This could be the end
and none of us knows

how to tell. Someone,
bored, unearths a book

along with the memo
on going paperless.

Like the Stem of a Thought Bubble

A trio of balloons caught
in the curmudgeon of a towering pine,
and I want to believe a nest
of fingers decided to let them go.
There could be messages
inside these red and yellow jellyfish
released to the wind current,
some secret confession fished
from a cloudless sky. Once,
a man tied enough to his lawn chair
to float for forty-five minutes.
Imagine flying high as an imagining,
the jet streams bearing him
ten years to the woods
where he aimed a gun at
the Hindenburg of his heart
the way he exploded each chamber
of helium to descend, his seat
saved at the Smithsonian,
still parked like those summers—
slam of car door, that tired weight
settled gratefully beneath the furious
reticule of California sunset.

Impressionism

> *"It is intoxicating to me, and I want to paint it all—*
> *my head is bursting…"*
> —Claude Monet

What a painting
it would make,

confetti of mind
burst from

the bone balloon
of his skull,

final masterpiece
to admire

from a distance
in some museum

to the dead,
knowing that when

you lean in
edges appear,

sharp and insistent
as a knife

on a table with
its study of fruit.

Jazz

Tonight I'm out of tune with knowing
the words, a refrain, bridges across.
Drop me in like a patron, like a man
off the street who didn't know
he was thirsty. Let the acrid snake
of smoke and sweat slither
its way into the horn of a throat
and I'll raise two fingers to the bar
as that high hat hiss constricts.
Oh jingle of ice in a glass,
I've become a reverb of days.
A discord, the sky a blues
of itself. Let this upright bass
begin its atrial fibrillation,
let fingers skitter to the heart key.
Play me like a trumpet—bent,
brassy and belled. Sharp, flat, all of it
all at once. Disassemble us,
put me back together. I'm begging
you. I'm a half-done harmony
and every song I swore I knew
I could never name.

V

Fog

Fog

So heavy this morning
to think it rained.
Last night's sorrow
hovering close,
another glistened eye?
The almost fall
you've tried and tried
to blink away?
Look to the river.
A sun's flawless lens
already at work
making the sight of
crumbled towns
clear.

Diagnosis: Eye Strain

I'll need special glasses, to filter blues.
Less fluorescent glare to glare into.
And every twenty minutes, the doctor says,
focus on something twenty feet away for
twenty seconds. It won't crystallize,
won't make everything perfect again.
That wall will resolve into a wall.
The parking lot outside your window
will still map out who is doing better.
Or worse, what has stayed between
the lines. But maybe it can ache
a diopter less, the way a hardness set
before you divides, is less solid,
a kind of ghost only kind of haunting
wherever you choose to look so long as
you choose to look through it.

MRI

When they ask about claustrophobia,
what they mean is: will lying in repose,
your arms crossed over your chest,
trigger certain feelings of dread?

When they ask about the one place
you would visit, what they're saying is:
will looking down this tunnel of light
at palm trees and white sand soothe you?

When they ask if you have metal
in your body, the question is: how
are you broken? Did you burst, rend
or rupture? What shattered inside?

If pale moons bloom and slide
ivory headlights across the wall
of your gray matter they'll say this:
incidental finding. It sounds unsinkable.

When they want to schedule another
one of these in six to nine months,
that radiologist is *overcautious.*
Otherwise it's all in your head.

Trouble Letting Go

Wait until you're alone.
Roll it up lovingly.
Carry it like a bride
through the front door.
Drive some back road
in the middle of the night
to a place you know or
will come to know as well
as a lover's body with all
its stone and imperfection.
Learn to let go of softness.
Cast it off like a ship
into dark waters along with
all the reasons to keep it.
If you have some time,
and the soil lifts just right,
give it a proper burial.
You owe it that much.

Going Back on the Pills

Friday of the first week of the first
ninety-day refill and I'm already paying
the price of readmission, have already
become the last of our peanut butter wrung
out of its hollowed jar, its tic-tac-toe
of desperate striations, the sound of it
stuck and strained through steel
across scorched dermises of bread.
Oh, but isn't that the process—
placing each empty vessel in the trash?
And later, with a little pat of luck,
a little therapy, into the recycling
before remembering like everyone else
to stop at the store for more,
that pleasure of choice—chunky,
smooth—laid out like an ailing road
they keep patching, releasing back
to the insanity of traffic.

Strange Look

Because it was your funeral again.
The part where, at the end
of his eulogy, your brother hit play,
where November Rain began
to slowly wash our bowed heads.
No fault of his that the speakers
could only handle a Liturgy's murmur,
the soft mull of ancient organs.
That Axl, even in the low registers,
could break a stereo of the divine word.
That one of us leaned over, cracked
the exact joke you should have whispered.
We quaked and cried how you'd always
made us, seated around long tables at lunch.
It's been a decade and still I'm your more
than willing marionette, corners of mouth
strung abruptly skyward, whole but stirred
with a darkness. That man in the car glancing
over like he wants to help, at the stoplight
as if it could be willed green.

October

The air begins to shrink into itself
like the skin of the starved,
and soon the graceful curve
of its rib will walk, hand in hand,
with the gnarled knuckle of winter.
But today, as you look up,
startled from raking's rhythm
by an unexpected kiss
to the back of your neck,
it's just a few frozen tears
flurrying from a passing sadness;
motes that linger but do not stick
to the drifts piled about your feet,
translucent beneath a glaze of sun,
the lines of their architecture
laid out like plans on the lawn,
thin and delicate as a bird's wing.

Male Pattern Baldness

Like an old belt with no holes to give
      I am unfastening.
It is a pale bridge connecting one continent
      to another and we
      are too stubborn to cross.
I'm unzipped teeth, a suitcase stuffed
      with too many goods of intention,
unglued like wallpaper in the closet
      we shove our baggage.
Ribbon curl and plaster's wan marrow
      beneath. On the dark side
      a moon waxes full.
In the mirror a receding tide.
      Dune grass bristles its sparse brush
where the salt wind combs and combs.

VI

What It Is

it is what it is

Isn't it always
what it is?
It is never not that.
It was what it is
and is as it was.
Perhaps you meant:
not what I wanted.
There's an expression
for that too.

On Halloween

I put on a mask,
hide myself twice over.

Superheroes pass by,
shoulder to shoulder with
their nemeses,

and the undead lurch
stolidly forward,
ragged under a sickle moon,

to stand in doorways
with the iridescent play
of fairy wings.

A whole legion of enemies
who have,
for one night,
laid down the sword.

Forgotten their hunger.

Imagine what could be
if, like them,

we tricked ourselves
into something sweeter.

Remodeling

for P & K

For ten years we cooked
ourselves into this place,
its linoleum warm with steps,
the air spiced by possibility,
and now as wallpaper rips
and the cabinets collapse
in a billow of white
I think of our friends,
up so late into the morning,
explaining why a family
sometimes remodels itself
smaller but never less,
how after they will pack up
his bowl, the water dish
so lovingly, the way I lowered
our life into boxes—
your grandmother's china,
my coffee mug,
a forgotten pepper mill—
the wiring exposed and raw,
how we go on working
and sleeping and eating until
the day you sense
the floor is level again,
and you will sit in something new
you've built for yourself,
and remember.

Stone Age

That year I would roam
around the new playground,
and beneath its canopy of wood
and steel hunt for lost tools.
Not ones fathers swore over,
their pull cord and coughing fits,
or the ominous glint of metal
brightening a barn wall.
No, in this fresh crush of rock
underfoot was the sharpness
that felled mammoths, that split
clear Pleistocene air like the blade
our teacher used to trim quizzes
and handouts, guillotine slow
and steady in practiced hands.
The many times I snuck back in
from recess early, a quarried stone
grasped in my fingers, and stopped
a private thought, an early lunch.
How he always lifted each arrowhead
or spear point to the fluorescent light,
saying *yes, this could be something.*

Having it Out with Winter

—after Jane Kenyon

1

It arrives with a weight,
so sodden you try to roll
a snowball and wring
water from water.

2

It breaks the extremities
of those who try to shoulder it,
redlines the heart's tachometer
of those who lift too much.

3

Listen to salt's gunfire
and for once melt
at that tunneling of one
into another.

4

They name it false spring,
these brief geysers welling up inside.

5

Those clouds will thicken,
will descend like a hydraulic press
to your head.

You eye them warily, for days.
Nothing falls.

6

It will visit the night
you've convinced yourself
of escape, will drift in on
the white noise of sleep.

7

The plow trawls the dark,
the glass fixtures in the living room
rattling as it strains
to keep the order of roads.

You dream of earthquakes,
of a blindness blown into your eyes
by an adversary.

8

Tumuli of snow—a car,
an overturned wheelbarrow.
The things you shoveled
from yourself.

9

Life's specter hung before you
like smoke. Diamonds rainbowed
over shoulders—a pinch from
all that has spilled.

December Moon

If there is some light at the end
of this tunnel let it not be
the day blind of living,
but this soft platter comforting
as the porcelain stacked in hutches
or on the wooden tongues
of buffets, the kind that says
quick, company is coming,
set your darkest table
with a few ragged napkins,
try not to bare the salt of stars.
Now let the scrupulous course
of the planets be served.
How nice it looks, chipped
and ancient thing dragged
across the endless ocean,
so worthless we forget
it is there, so necessary
we gave it a face.

Mother is a Verb, too

I watch you follow a friend's daughter,
her ride home after a shift at the restaurant.
It's a school night, snowing. Mom is
working the graveyard so I watch you watch
their pale blue dot on your phone wheel
through the astrometry of youth: empty lot,
donuts, eight of anything such an inconceivable
number they topple it sideways, carve infinity
symbols in front of a bookstore. When you call,
she'll say it was the friend's idea, tell you it
is *so terrifying*, the looping out and back like
a comet, insides shaken, the maraca of forces.
How like us they almost managed to let go,
almost slid out into spaces between light.
Always just enough grip, enough to
lose control again.

VII

Braiding

Relax

—after Ellen Bass

Good things will happen.
Your lost dog will be found,
the long line of its leash
trailing like an afterthought.
Your superstitions will work.
The knocked wood walks
off the ninth, closes out the game.
Your mom will text. The scan
shows his lungs. Nothing else.
Miracle will pry apart your lips.
Yes, you will forget one small bud
bringing in geraniums before a frost.
Yes, your wife will haul anchor
after anchor of you up from the muck
into her arms. Remember Ariadne?
How she saves a man from his labyrinth.
Her cleverness, her length of thread
he stitches to that lonely island.
In one version she hangs herself.
In another marries a god. Embrace it.
Not the god. I mean toes curled in sand,
this sunset yours. A coconut will fall
and you won't be thirsty. The seed,
so small and fetal in the unfurled palm,
bursting like a minotaur from dirt.
Yes, it roars, there are days enough.
Days the rope dangles, open-mouthed,
speechless in a sail filling wind.

Braiding the Challah

> *To them God can only appear as bread and butter.*
> —*Mahatma Gandhi*

The voyeur in me wants
to watch you knead it
the way a lifeguard pushes
the sea out of lungs fished
from a spume of waves,
as a surgeon must sometimes
reach in and massage the heart.
I want to press my ear
to the door and hear the prayers
you were taught spill
from your gentile tongue
as one braid twines
around the other like legs
in love's acclamation.
Such things are necessary
as bread, and as it lies
in oven's confessional we
can contemplate this kitchen,
your grandmother's spoon
flashing from the mixing bowl
like a relic in its sunbeam.
I too want to know resurrection.
How miracles can just be recipes
of unlike stuffs stirred smooth.
Coming home tonight I smell it
hung on your hair like a scarf—
nondenominational, the millennia
that rise and hold what is placed
without crumbling.

February

Now days throw off the blanket
of early morning snow by noon.

Shovels idle against the house,
wide bellied workmen.

You read of a famous poet
who, after graduation,

dropped everything to study
Buddhism for eight years.

It's too early for gardening,
too late for exposure.

You sleep fitfully,
go to movies on the weekend.

You think of the Buddha's wife
and son, crying in the dark.

The bloated belly of absence.
Washing dishes after dinner,

you hear for the first time
birds singing.

Rerouted

What a peculiar delight
to discover there are still buses
marking these neighborhoods
like long yellow highlighters,
every small body obscured
by its backpack an equally
important text burdened
beneath the weight of learning.
That primary lesson: knowledge
is heavy. And it is heavy,
how the current popular kids
still claim the stern, those same
stylish clothes they'll outgrow
in a matter of months—
pristine sneakers, hats unmarred
by hand-me-down-ness,
pearlescent teeth sandwiching
tongues pink as wild caught salmon
aimed downstream at you.
Still, one can find comfort knowing
there is a hierarchy above seating
arrangements, how small kindnesses
and alliances will butter these
beltless brown nooks, perhaps across
a lifetime. The way one confidant
who sat with you in the middle row
asks in that low do you think she likes me
tone about an illness you both share.
The hurt, he says, when will it go
away, resolve? It's the first time
the best friend of a body has failed,
let down. And what could you say?
What wisdom fallen like Pez
from the dispenser of your mouth,
you who are sticking your own tongue
out now, your hands like antlers
plugged into the side of your head,
trading faces with a popularity
one fifth your age? Because sometimes

that's all that matters in a given
moment—forgetting your paunch,
the commute lengthened by construction
making you late for what you call work.
Like your lined, ridiculous mug for them
something to remember when pain—
everyone's secret crush—slips again softly
into this open seat beside you.

The Handshake

For years my father enveloped
a ball with his hand,
lifted iron in his down time
at work with iron intent.
His grip ferrous, gnarled,
knurled as each dropped barbell.
Once, I asked him to show me
and my fingers welded,
a billet I shook for hours after
as if part of me too had died,
demanded restoration.
And now that I have reached
that age, I still don't know why
we do this, why men hold on
not wanting to be the first
released. As if creating
diamonds in their palms.
Once, an interviewer observed
I possessed a woman's grasp.
As we detached and I walked out
of his office, I thought of
another mistake passed long ago.
Of two women—one younger,
one silvered with age—also set
apart. How, as the tow truck
hefted the tattered front
of a minivan onto itself,
they reached out to shake
but collided again, forehead
to forehead, whispering.
God, if ever by accident
I careen back into this life,
let me agitate all the hands
just like a woman.

I, too, Love Lucy

though I've never watched your show.
Never been high on highballs,
the big band's brass,
that atmosphere of secondhand smoke.
Still, there are times I pause,
pacing head down through this house.
The shadow box of you there,
its glamour hung from the wall
our one outrageous expense.
Stepping out of a show in Vegas,
first vacation since the funeral,
something lifted from our shoulders.
One hand found the other, it was alien.
We walked to not let go until
she stopped—*let's take a look.*
Lucy, you would have had a ball
in there, all that memorabilia laid out
like an overpriced graveyard.
You would have known half the store.
We found you in the very back—
red heart candy box, you in your iconic
toque, that facemask of chocolate,
smooth ribbons of signature.
Lucy, can I confide something?
I'm falling asleep to Star Trek again.
They're stuck in a time loop, again.
And there are times we all want out.
Is it a taking if you know you're reborn?
Because Lucy, I'm still in love
with warped fields, how any humanoid
feels their déjà vu of given days,
the way they dilate to years.
Tell me you haven't longed to beam,
be reassembled off world.
What I'm saying is I'm loving you
in the most selfishly sapiens way.
Like a rerun, like this rip in the continuum
because you boldly greenlit a marriage

of pilots instead of the usual one—
The Cage and *Where No Man
Has Gone Before.*

Henge

Here the sleepy eye
of east facing window
catches early spring sun,
there a broken blind
juliennes light across
the cutting board of wall.
Here is an unmade bed,
here is you sloshing
up out of the dream tide
to the mortal porthole
strung with photons,
an almost music.
And when you are there,
the groggy shoreline
of waking reduced to ash,
you will finally glean
that impulse to alignment,
why they invested
so much for a glance,
that single golden thread
drawn through an eyehole
of rock each solstice.
Why we've always patched,
stitched or hemmed this way,
the precarious thinness
in our thick and meaty fingers,
two edges drawn closed
like a mouth opened to speak
deciding against it.

Bodybuilder

Too heavy, too old,
this once reusable bag body
that more often now feels
like an I forgot to do the things
that keep it here body so
it became a five-cent surcharge,
a paper constitution rending
its wet-self open, puddling
parking lots, a sidewalk,
waterfalling long staircases
from apartments to the street,
a disemboweled body,
all the things you move its
begrudging mass for bruised
or burst, bodies broken
beyond repair, no antibody
for this forgetfulness,
this electric singing body
bending without second thought
beside you, how it hugs
what was pronounced dead
into the cavity that makes every
body a body of work,
and able.

Another Dollar Store

The day before
they break ground
I see a man onsite
digging up lupines.
He's done this before,
the way he binds
each ache of dusk
and plum in burlap,
a bruise of beauty
secreted away
in the trunk
of an old Subaru
I'll see parked
the next morning
by a bulldozer.

Acknowledgments

The author gratefully acknowledges the editors and readers of the following online and print publications in which the poems below first appeared (some in slightly different versions):

"Putting it Off," *Panoply*
"Old Piano," *Pirene's Fountain*
"The Weeding," *Rat's Ass Review*
"Nest," *Pirene's Fountain*
"In the Photo," *Thimble*
"A Long Dead Spider," *Poetry Village*
"Spring Noir," *Sandy River Review*
"Hand Axe," *Bracken*
"Dermatology," *Black Nore Review*
"Heart Monitor," *Deep Water Series, edited by Megan Grumbling*
"Red or White," *Black Nore Review*
"Mathura Man Sets Record by Staring at Sun for Over an Hour," *Rattle's Poets Respond*
"Fine Print," *Deep Water Series, edited by Megan Grumbling*
"Schrödinger's Office," *Hole in the Head Review*
"Humidity," *Pirene's Fountain*
"Power Outage: Office," *Rust + Moth*
"Impressionism," *The Lake*
"Diagnosis: Eye Strain," *Rust + Moth*
"Trouble Letting Go," *Frost Meadow Review*
"Going Back on the Pills," *Hole in the Head Review*
"October," *Aurorean*
"Remodeling," *Sandy River Review*
"Male Pattern Baldness," *Sandy River Review*
"Stone Age," *Frost Meadow Review*
"Braiding the Challah," *Finest (by Ben Banyard)*
"February," *The Lake*
"Another Dollar Store," *Clear Poetry*
"Mother is a Verb, too," *Panoply*
"Dave," *Clear Poetry*
"On Halloween," *Poetry Breakfast*

Originally from Las Vegas, **Gus Peterson** grew up in Massachusetts and has lived in Maine for over twenty years. He serves on the board of the Maine Poets Society, a nonprofit dedicated to bringing poetry to all Mainers. Work has appeared online in *Rust + Moth, Bracken, Thimble, ONE Art*, and in print with *Pirene's Fountain*. A chapbook, *When the Poetry's Gone,* was released by Encircle Publications in 2015. He resides in an old farmhouse with his beloved, Carol, a stone's throw from the Kennebec River. This is his first full length collection.

www.ingramcontent.com/pod-product-compliance
Lightning Source LLC
Chambersburg PA
CBHW030055170426
43197CB00010B/1529